I used to
love you

I used to love you

by Emilia Mlak

Published by Emilia Mlak

www.tiktok.com/@artemimla

www.instagram.com/llamateurs/

to all of you who
love
hurt
fall
and come back again

thank you for choosing to read this book
it takes you through life's ups and downs
moments of passion, fury, helplessness and
hope

this is what happens when
you listen to stories
and pour them onto paper
creating fiction
inspired by truth

contents

the love

meeting you

we've met on a cold day
in coffee shop
you looked up and waved
I had to stop

the warmth of your voice
and smell of the place
inviting moment
so pleasant to taste

you seemed to be cheeky
but not underneath
so neatly hiding
the feelings beneath

I sensed your devotion
I knew you were home
one fragile sentence
I'm totally blown

some awkward silence
a cringe then a laugh
two hours later
I am your half

not fit to human codes

I sense how you look at me
I sense what you
want to see
I sense I am not your lot
I sense what you need is
hot

I'm out of my comfort zone
you move and I'm
almost gone
I'm scared
but I'm also high
you touch and I almost
die

the crossing of our roads
will
not fit to human codes

the outer and inner space
will always resemble
this place

can't think

your words are warm
but breath is much
warmer
I hear your voice
but brain
ate its corner

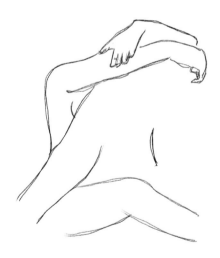

the spinning

vertigo
contigo
I don't need any words

the space is closing round
the words are turning sound

the spinning of eternal
the face goes geothermal

we chase anatomical
the hands out of typical

the burning sense of taste
the hunger and the haste

we lay under the sweat
when our bodies
met

vocal cord

your laugh is like a path
the vocal
cord
soft and clear
through the fjord

I caught it

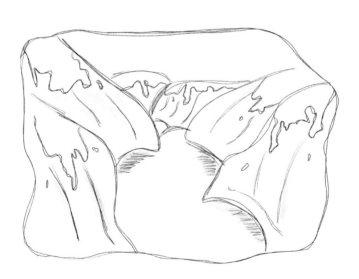

open

keeping close to your
charms
keeping close to world's
arms
this time it's real
not in my mind
the wavy tail
of beauty
will blind

here and now

I can giggle
I can smile
all I ask for
please don't die

colliding

the big bang must admit
we're kinda
lost a bit
the effort to create
has sealed our final fate

the heat
the beat
the blow
the speed of choking show
the urge of
being close
was born at core and rose

we seem to know the facts
we seem to know who acts
the photons
they don't need
to know their final speed

the moments they do
crash
in nanosecond flash
the only certain thing
is how
your eyes can sing

perfect blur

my vision got blurred
cause you
occurred
perfection is
lost
I'm lost to the cost

and it's so perfect

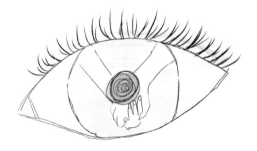

leaf story

can you feel the green leaf
that has fallen from dark
no sense of direction
no knowledge of mark
I marked
your abundance
the way the leaf does
secretly flying
away
from the mass

you have been chosen
no matter the gloss
the leaf could fly further but flew
heart across
it opened the green veins
it caught right away
adhesive nature
my quiet display

I'm touching your arm
please notice my glance
if leaf returns you
will I have a chance?
the eyes are
connecting
the sudden outburst
of need and belonging
we can be cursed

please never leave me
please never stop
I've never felt this
you're leaf -
I'm a drop
symbiosis of goings
you fly -
I can sink
a perfect structure
like eye and its blink

the snow

you rescued me like a hero
from books
you covered my lines
away
from the looks
I'm grateful forever
it's not nothing
you know
when left peripheral
and someone
warms snow

forming

counting days to meeting you
bought a dress
champagne
"I do"

warmer nights
a sun
the rain
on the table
us
then stain

calming storms
compartment fight
love in all its
forming might

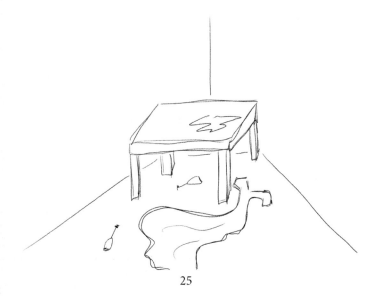

learning curve

touching your face
every time
like final embrace
in her prime

forest

spontaneous kinds we are
we jump into your car
adventure
close to home
we're born to
run and roam

the slightest break of must
we feed our inner
lust
a forest full of dark
a dog who starts to bark

and in these silent smells
a net of rooting cells
we play now
hide and seek
that's how our bodies
speak

daily chore

and if now marks forever
I'll hold you tight
my sweet
endeavour

tattoo

the rays of your
blissful smile
have entered my inner aisle
it's spreading – the sweetest
disease
I'm breaking to every kiss

I'm yours
and you know it well
I've shed my courageous shell
I nod to no questions
and eyes
I am lost in not being
wise

I'm holding your body
so close
the heat burns your cheeks
and my clothes
a mixture
of pigments and oils
is melting my heart as it
boils

and it bursts with emotions I hid
and it pours with no dam or a lid
I am done
I surrender to you
I'm your ink
you're my deepest tattoo

directions

north or south
I don't know
all I know is
don't go slow

the vine

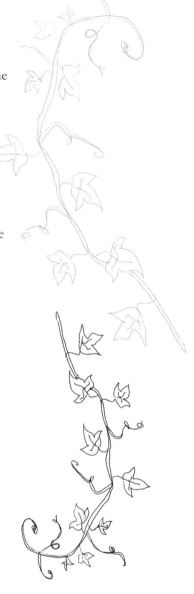

the moment your sparkle met mine
that moment created a
vine
a green lash of cadence and
life
the quick snaps of
future as wife

the reasons we gladly escape
the combats we hide near the cape
and all we went on
and through
this all have created
anew

we nod to the yes and no
we hit of the lowest
low
and then when it's
quiet and near
we lose our clothing
severe

amazed with the colours of
vine
we swear to
what's yours is mine
embraced with the power of
love
it's all I can think of

down there

the hands
they seek
you press
I peak

I'm grateful

I sink my hand in
the more and within
I couldn't care less
if we are a mess

I've waited so long
to dream and belong
you gave it to me
and I let it free

I'm grateful

tomorrow

we live aside as team
we share another's dream
we bathe in morning's flesh
we kiss our lips afresh

we meet another line
and then the other
nine
we used to understand
the easiest way to mend

it's not an easy task
to stay with
self
not mask
to do it as a pair
an overwhelming share

to talk and be and live
as two
is not a give
you can you know you do
until you have no clue

as sharpened as an eye
the sense of being
mine
I'll sink to it today
tomorrow might not may

I'm not concerned

I've done my part
I left my
heart
it's yours to pick
and give a
kick

this time it's slow
colliding show
what's real in me
it's yours to
free

don't be afraid
release my
wait
and guide me through
the deepest you

I'm not concerned

the fading

●

killing me softly
I heard this song

anthill

I saw atomic whirl
yes
that kind of girl
I see the things you don't
but doesn't mean
you won't

if we were to
lay down
on warm and grassy
crown
if we were to stay close
I need to know
you chose

to see the ground and ants
who start the day with chants
who end life with a sigh
not willed to say
goodbye

you've earned
the life to live
you can and will
forgive
the strength is to be learnt
too late
– the anthill burnt

clever

we're clever enough to
jump
but how high
is the ramp

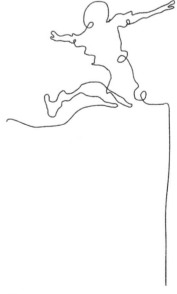

scar

I'm here
you're here
we are

crack

let's rip another scar

bus

must I insist
to be on your side
must I persist
to let this one slide

I haven't touched you
for so long –
admit
you don't really bother
we're such in deep sh*t

I could have cursed you
believe me
I tried
but was it worth it
to be times denied

I wanted mirage
I wanted
us
instead our love

was hit by a bus

really

do you really know
what it's really like
when you really hang
on a really spike
when it really tears
whole your really part
how I really hate
me
with all my heart

keeper's thing

keep going
keep down
keep watching
keep bow
keep open
keep lost
keep chosen
keep frost
keep moving
keep clock
keep meaning
keep shock
keep greeting
keep up

the keeper's thing…
we are all f***ed

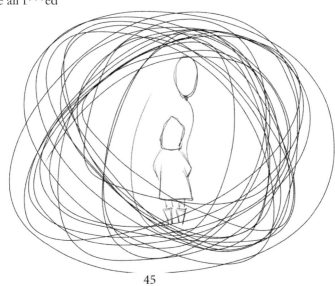

dead ends

another talk
with dead ends we know
I seek advantage
at all costs
so low

I dig so hollow
I reach underground
no good
or agreement
can rise here or mount

you stare with
your pained look
you can't find the words
I break them with
sables
good luck dear
try swords

we're not on
arena
for people to cheer
your look getting
dimmer
I'm getting lost here

why not defending
your reasons
your rights
no matter hurting
the new level heights?

you can't even look now
I'm getting a sense
after this dead end
you're changing the lens

●

begging

place me inside your head
otherwise mine is
dead

just one

so many ways
to express raging
cry
but escape is handing
a glass of red wine

warm pier

I asked you over
again and again
you kept chilling
silence
I knew where to grey

I brew my own
sentence
on warm pier in may
I felt all those
ice winds
again and again

another breakfast
on shy
tingling wood
the perfect
exhausting
disturbance of good

I knew something happens
when crossing the line
when reaching too gently
for only and
mine

I know all the comfort
of being the one
when slowly but
surely
I'm ready to run

●

another sentence
another wood
again and again
the what ifs and would

us

I go
you try
I beg
you cry
too soon
too far
two hearts
one lie

am I

are the meanings flawed
am I sometimes fraud
bringing into life
happy place with
knife

am I sometimes weird
placing your long beard
in my mind to hide
hiding's mine
that's right

do you dim your eyes
to my net of lies
scratching on the floor
is my favourite chore

when you hold me close
it's another dose
of my fear to trust
so I'm choosing
past

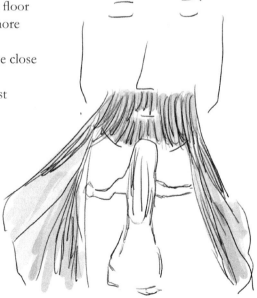

ghost choices

misunderstandings
are food for tries
another lover
your bed
my lies

we keep it
simple
no reason to brag
another reason
or reason to drag

these are our
choices
so many I'm lost
this one is
different
becoming a ghost

and it will haunt us
in prisons of *let's*
difficult challenge
full of
regrets

if we survive this
my dear and the one
we're doomed to whisper
the harm has been done

one touch

it's been a longer
while
since I've seen your smile
press my hand with touch
we just need that
much

flu

I don't know
but will I ever
if our cast is shaped
forever

you have
doubts
but will you ever
understand
I'm not that clever

I can catch your vague ideas
I can hold to how you see us
I can sail through
your
own
mind
if our thoughts are still aligned

I read book
you take your time
kitchen smells of
sweat and thyme
I feel better
after you
please stay closer
love's a flu

chances

will we be
or will be tree
will roots rot
or have a shot

safe distance

likeness
protrusion
I better leave

I kept all the
distance
I let myself grieve

I sewed you
I rode you
you never complained

until from
tomorrow
the tissues were grained

likeness
illusion
I better stay

when all the
distance
becomes a safe bay

awe

I looked at the sky
and it shook me
with eternity of signs
with courageous clouds
I could watch with awe

have a lawn to mow

floor

I put my best to us and wait
I put my chest to floor
at eight
we glide together
even shine
the winding precious softest
pine

we lay together
arm in arm
we face no obvious cheated
harm
the tear of joy
the tear of trust
the saddest floor who felt the
lust

my dearest
floor
my dear old friend
you lay out hardest living hand
I reach to grab it
I reach and
fall
you understand and
hug me whole

it's all I needed
all I asked
you were my nurture
and morning's blast
I stand up slowly
divided mind
the sweetest comfort
of a kind

seagull

I walk along your side
and plant another tide
of pressure and remorse
a sudden change of course

we used to play it safe
we used to calm the wave
this time a grip of sand
creates the driest land

I'm fighting with the wind
my cry is somehow thinned
I catch a tear of pain
and then it starts to
rain

your ears have heard enough
we're close to losing path
the seagull
  ate
   my
    voice
I think I've made a choice

shall we

do you feel it?
no I don't
do you mean it?
no I won't
can we talk?
I wish I could
shall we stop?
I think we should

hopes unheard

I haven't
I didn't
or maybe have I?

you didn't notice
anyway
bye

be kind to yourself

I'm old
to be
I'm old
to me
I'm old
enough
I'm old
for rough
I'm old
with you
I'm old
like you
I'm old and
 kind

to leave my mind

the things we do

I dare you
you sigh
the conscious escapism of thigh

I read you
you smirk
the intimate power of quirk

I claw you
you lit
the roughest combustion of fit

I call you
you smile
the toughest goodbye in a while

I used to love you

I used to love you
but now I
don't
I used to love you
leftover clot

you used to love me
it wasn't hard
I used to love
back
with all my heart

with all this using
and pumping blood
we reached the purest
amazing
mud

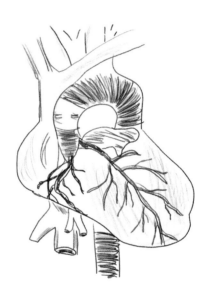

it ate my finger
your body
our air
pure love was standing
aside with a stare

and when consumed
and entirely
gone
I used to love you
like others
till dawn

agony

you let it all go
I let it all out
we never knew how
loud
we could shout

the stairs up and down
the lock
and the key
is there a reason how
far
we should be?

the glass and the dog
the rain and your gloom
the love and
the hate –
a part of this room

a dinner
you cook
I'm cooking your fate
there's no illusion
this time it's too late

and in an hour
or maybe in two
you lose your
senses
I'll cut them too

and in a day
or maybe in two
you say
I'm sorry
I feel it too

and in a week
or maybe
a month
we cross the street
to say
I'm fine

and in a year
or maybe three
we both live in this
agony

the act

pill

catatonic tones
spreading through my bones
pill
is what I've got
pill
will help a lot

customs

monsters
have been created to scare
by people with
nothing to declare

but they really do
have something

I swear

I know I'm not ok
the rules I
must obey

are countless in the dark
my will
has curved to arc

I'm somehow
still alive
we play a man and
wife

I'm dusting my old self
with cleaning cloth on shelf

the photos in the frames
resembling more
obeys
are screaming loud and clear
another
painful year

I've cheated on myself
here comes another shelf

a shattered glass on floor
I swear there will be
more

doubts

changing
raging
am I proud?

no
I'm pure
and selfish
doubt

to where and who

and here I go
with stick and
saw
with no conclusion
full of illusion

over and over
the time turned
sober
if only we could
blind eyes for
good

the wheel is rolling
you keep up going
to where and who
there's no
pass through

she kept on trying
they left her
dying
to where and who
the answer is
you

●

paranoia

I don't know today
different vibe
dismay
better eat the thoughts
better burn the knots

I can't sleep with touch
I can't eat too much
itching
witching
cut
what is me
what not

button

it's so dark now
where's the light
have I lost
half of sight

fear at nine
life at three
which direction
head will free

could be stronger
could *be fine*
I'm in claws of
misalign

found my prayer
found my cause
will my brain press
button *pause*

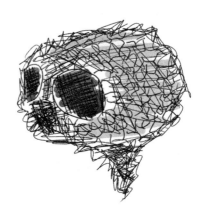

neighbour

somebody's watching
an old man from eight
I hear him judging
two minutes too late

her

I escaped
a thousandth time today
my thoughts restricted
my mouth
bleeding prey
I wanted freedom
I didn't ask for much
it turned out
different
a hunting of a such

we wanted laughters
the endless melting hoarse
we're digging slowly
a place
for ready corpse

no one can rescue
no one can see
what's going to happen

can she

monster

raging fury all inside
I'm not ready
breathe and hide
scary monster
go away
leave my world
free my day

going mad now
please let go
final say
bare and raw
I don't need you
I deny
you took all
what's dear or mine

have a mercy
devil's son
it's all over
I am done
have no strength
to fight your stay
self invited
I'm your prey

sit and feast
on shattered parts
tired cells
have come to guard

what remained
of me and us
will prevail
beneath the grass

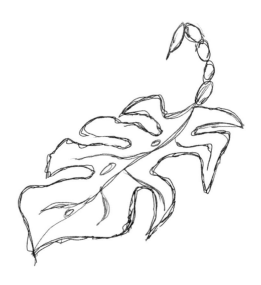

●

can't

can't sleep
can't walk
can't rush
can't talk
can't eat
can't try
you're here to
die

life

why
does it feel so
heavy

creatures

I don't agree
to what I see
to what I break
to what you take

you dreadful creature
you sucked my air

you crept in slowly
on thinner hair

I can't control
you filled my veins
and you're so close
to win my brains

I don't agree
I had enough
release my
sentence
I can take rough

10am

I hide today
It's not my day
I'm half asleep
I'll take a sip

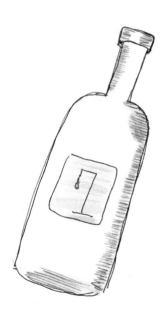

●

the act

no no no
not this time
you built ashes
I grew crime
you will never sleep again
I'm your prison
you're my main

I will toss you
taste and
run
I will throw away your sun
I will promise to
my world
you will never get a hold

sound of water
washing blood
with majestic laughing god
me and mirror –
final stage
pictures phrases
maniac rage

steps to freedom
touching hand
I've been waiting my old friend
hug me more you've ever tried
until all my senses
die

allegation to sane

I don't need to
remember
the sea or the beach
I know we can hold hands

or pour on them bleach

the sane are the same
they're scared or
they know
pretending to check when

you're dinner for crow

what happens in hive stays there

bee bee
me
bee bee
sting
moods for
everlasting
drink

bee bee
fly
bee bee
die
come and go
the waves
in hive

bee bee
most
bee bee
lost
nothing changes
all is
moist

I used to love you

●

the act vol 2

inspiration
deviation
bitter time has come for us

you can hold
truth be told
rage unmildly squeezing pus

all these years
are gone for
hers
taming water reaching max

words were spoken
pain as token
no I won't and
try relax

head is spinning
devil's grinning
she has stolen precious part

I will find her
I will kill her
justice served
with all my
heart

...

so much peace now
I can't see –
how?
scarlet liquid warming face

next time you dear
now it's so clear
thank you gods for all your grace

●

one morning

I woke up to
hate you
I woke up to
trade you
I woke up to
lose us
I woke up to
use gas

he saw

the old man who spoke
the old man who died
the old man who never looked in the eye

the old man he knew
the old man he lied
the old man who never will see the sky

the old man he felt
the old man he cried
the old man who never will pass by

the old man who spoke
the old man who died
the old man who never will ask
why

done

sweet tooth
sweet mine
the fairy can come

and take it away
I'll check
if it's done

obotomy

he smell
he loss
a mad lady who walked across

he paper
he pen
reception room full of them

the look
the face
a door knob increases pace

we're here
we're close
a nurse hands another dose

I'm locked
I vent
I promise a full repent

why now
what for
lie down
it's time to explore

97

the new me

olfactory organ

somebody once told me
your voice is so strong
I could just sit here
and stare all day long

I'm staring at voice now
I'm struggling to speak
this world will devour
your senses if weak

I switch to my smell then
it holds dearest scent
of me from before
and what my voice meant

and now I feel power
as I cough through my nose
my voice tells slowly
only what smell knows

letter

I wrote a letter
to my own self
I think it started when I was
twelve
I brought a smile to school that day
and came back home so
far away

I've painted pictures
for friends for fun
nobody knew it was my run

I have escaped so many times
to warmth of colours
and mellow lines

I smiled
at school
at work
at home
my children laughing
I'm not alone

but in the deepest secret room
I dared to wilt and fade the bloom

I sketched my face
a wrinkle part
I stitched my head
it wasn't hard

out in a letter
a wrinkled page
has seen it all
the fall and the
rage

my hood

when I was little girl
I never understood
why all my classmates glared
and I sat in my hood

when I was bigger girl
I dared to send a smile
but it was wrongly dared
the boy soon said goodbye

when I was teenage girl
I felt explosive match
but soon a lesson learnt
I'm not enough to touch

and now I'm finally me
I'm old enough to see
the hood was heavy night
a tool to see the light

healing

how am I supposed to break
if I don't know how to take
all these people
all at once
I'm in bubble
but can't bounce

from the glassy sparkling walls
I am calling through the holes
they can't hear it
now I'm stuck
can't go forward
can't go back

I am breaking suddenly
my voice trembling
hard to see
all the heads now turn around
I am crying
lost to sound

grave

I take a shovel
I feel the wind
my feelings
gone
suppressed
binned
I dig a hole
I dig so hard
my hands
worn
dirty
unbalmed

the art of strength
the art of truth
the feeling of overwhelming
sooth

to dig is one
to grieve is two
bye bye
my part of being you

acceptance

it's hard
but true
I'm not
with you

let go

hope is there
I saw a flare
on calm wide sea
I swam to
me

this time is real
I finally feel
a quiet star
comes back from
afar

I touch the flare now
I softly allow
the motion to
flow
the mind to go slow

there's no aiming to
there's no going through
it's gentle as
shock
to let go of block

whenever

watch your pain
ready to listen
whenever

letting in

the people are a map
they are your safety cap
if you just let them in
they're better than a gin

born to

oh my
I finally understand
why
I couldn't dare to walk
I couldn't even talk

I felt so smoothly passed
the faces were too vast
the ovals went too long
I'm finally growing
strong

I'm facing everyday
I know it's now okay
to ask and take a hand
when I'm in nowhere land

it's drastic of a kind
to dare to speak your mind
to listen and reply
to make your neurons
fry

but I'm my better
choice
I come from deepest voice
I've been here long enough
to know I'm born to
laugh

time

time will seal
time will heal

trust issues

let go
just breathe
and drop the sheath
I'm here to help
I hear your
yelp

I hug you tight
with all my might
you're not
alone
I am your own

just trust

rebound

so many people
have walked through my path
for some I am grateful
from some I need bath

but the experience
in all wildest forms
survived the weakest
gained strength through the storms

I'm not an exception
I know we are here
to tell different stories
to shed someone's tear

together we're bigger
we reach through the ground
eroded rocks give space
to rebound

safe place

you're not alone
you know
don't you?
your head is hurt
allow me to
stitch up the wound
it's fresh and
deep
you're safest when
allowed to weep

you're sad so much
I cry along
together now
tomorrow strong

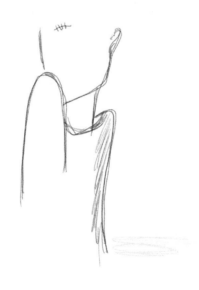

not part of when
you hide
pretend
the strongest part is
when you bend

and when the streams have
dried your face
the demons dropped
and stopped the chase
I look at head
the stitch is there
your baggage safe
between brown hair

so little and so much

let's just
sit together

adjusting sight

you're not alone
don't overthink
just turn your eye around
and blink

secret

I left this feeling long time ago
comeback is healing
but also burns low

I reach out for present
it turns out to be
my little secret
it's yours to see

nobody's different and also the same
I see your contours
the beam of shame
it is your treasure
my motion
your glue
are you aware of holding right through?

I talk to you
gently
no reason to hide
nobody's different

you are the light

You are.

this blank page is
for you
to let go
and
breathe through

I used to love you

thank you expression
so simple but rare
you think it's nothing
I know you care

Instagram: www.instagram.com/llamateurs/

TikTok: @artemimla

or visit her website:

www.linktr.ee/artemimla

Support the author and leave a review on Amazon!
Just scan this QR code:

Thanks!

Printed in Great Britain
by Amazon

58260846R00076